STECK-VAUGHN
PORTRAIT OF AMERICA

New Jersey

Steck-Vaughn Company

Executive Editor	Diane Sharpe
Senior Editor	Martin S. Saiewitz
Design Manager	Pamela Heaney
Photo Editor	Margie Foster

Proof Positive/Farrowlyne Associates, Inc.
Program Editorial, Revision Development, Design, and Production

Consultant: Howard L. Green, New Jersey Historical Commission

Published by Raintree Steck-Vaughn Publishers, an imprint of Steck-Vaughn Company.

A Turner Educational Services, Inc. book. Based on the Portrait of America television series by R. E. (Ted) Turner.

Cover Photo: Cape May Victorian homes by © Joe Sohn/The Stock Market.

Library of Congress Cataloging-in-Publication Data

Thompson, Kathleen.
    New Jersey / Kathleen Thompson.
        p.   cm. — (Portrait of America)
    "Based on the Portrait of America television series"—T.p. verso.
    "A Turner book."
    Includes index.
    ISBN 0-8114-7375-9 (library binding).—ISBN 0-8114-7456-9 (softcover)
    1. New Jersey—Juvenile literature. I. Title. II. Series:
Thompson, Kathleen. Portrait of America.
F134.3.T46   1996
974.9—dc20   95-22846
                                                           CIP
                                                           AC

Printed and Bound in the United States of America

   3   4   5   6   7   8   9   10   WZ   03   02   01   00

Acknowledgments
The publishers wish to thank the following for permission to reproduce photographs:
P. 7 © Superstock; p. 8 North Wind Picture Archives; p. 11 © Dorothy Toulson; p. 12 Morristown National Historical Park, NPS; p. 13 The Bettmann Archive; p. 15 The Passaic County Historical Society; p. 16 The Bettmann Archive; p. 17 Edison National Historic Site, NPS; p. 18 The Passaic County Historical Society; p. 19 New Jersey Turnpike Authority; pp. 20–23 Edison National Historic Site, NPS; p. 24 © Michael Reagan; p. 26 (top) Courtesy New Jersey Division of Travel & Tourism, (bottom) The Port Authority of New York and New Jersey; p. 27 © Superstock; p. 28 Pfizer Inc.; p. 29 AT&T Bell Laboratories; pp. 30 & 31 Courtesy New Jersey Division of Travel & Tourism; p. 32 photo courtesy of the Mid-Atlantic Center for the Arts; p. 34 Paper Mill Playhouse; p. 35 (top) Courtesy New Jersey Division of Travel & Tourism, (bottom) UPI/Bettmann; p. 36 Atlantic City Convention & Visitors Authority; p. 37 (top) Atlantic City Convention & Visitors Authority, (bottom) MONOPOLY®, the gameboard, and certain of its elements and playing pieces are registered trademarks of Tonka Coroporation. Used with Permission. © 1935, 1946, 1961, 1992, 1994 Parker Brothers, a division of Tonka Corporation. All rights reserved.; p. 38 © Gilbert Mika/New Jersey State Park Service; p. 39 (left) New Jersey State Park Service, (right) © Gilbert Mika/New Jersey State Park Service; p. 40 Clean Ocean Action/Roosevelt Environmental Club; p. 41 Clean Ocean Action; p. 42 AT&T Bell Laboratories; p. 44 The Emilio Segrè Visual Archives; p. 46 One Mile Up; p. 47 (top left) One Mile Up, (top right) Courtesy New Jersey Division of Travel and Tourism.

STECK-VAUGHN
PORTRAIT OF AMERICA

New Jersey

Kathleen Thompson

A Turner Book

RSVP

RAINTREE
STECK-VAUGHN
PUBLISHERS
The Steck-Vaughn Company

Austin, Texas

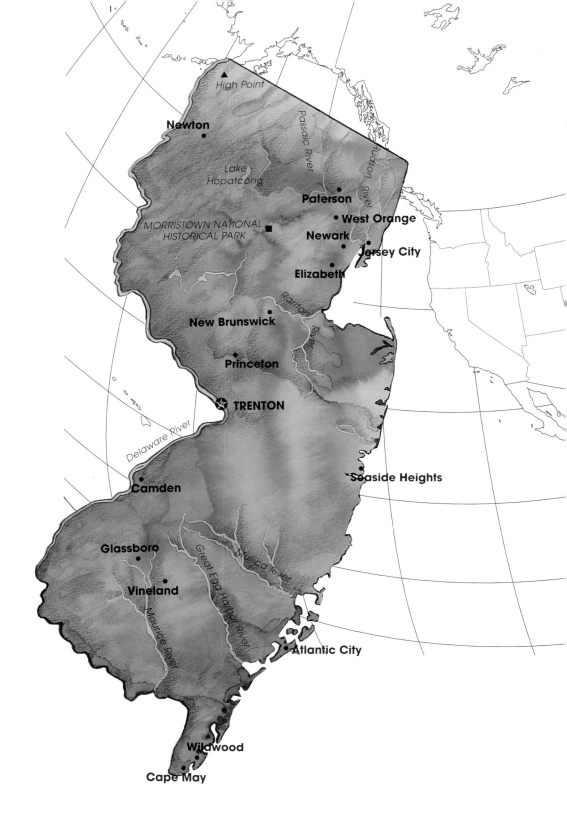

New Jersey

High Point ▲

Newton •

Lake
Hopatcong

Passaic River

Paterson •
• West Orange

MORRISTOWN NATIONAL
HISTORICAL PARK ■

Newark •

Jersey City

Elizabeth •

Hudson River

New Brunswick •

Raritan River

Princeton •

⬡ TRENTON

Delaware River

Seaside Heights •

Camden •

Glassboro •

Great Egg Harbor River

Mullica River

Vineland •

Maurice River

Atlantic City •

Wildwood •

Cape May •

Contents

Introduction

It's easy to think of New Jersey as being on the way to somewhere else. Like the hub of a wheel, it is crisscrossed by transportation lines. They lead not only east to New York City and west to Philadelphia, but to the north and south as well. Yet New Jersey is much more than a stop on the way to somewhere else. Those who stop to look find a cornucopia—a seemingly magical horn of plenty spilling out both the fruits of its factories and the fruits of the land. But the key to this small state's productivity isn't magic. It is people—and New Jersey has more people per square mile than any other state. Though it boasts mountains, forests, and seashores, New Jersey's most valuable resource is the energy and ingenuity of its people. Their hard work supplies the nation with every-thing from roses to medicines, from cranberries to computers.

Atlantic City, New Jersey, attracts thirty million tourists each year. They come to visit hotels, restaurants, casinos, shops, and theaters on the city's famous Boardwalk.

New Jersey

From the Lenni-Lenape to Atlantic City

New Jersey, which has a population of about seven and three quarters of a million people, was once the home of eight thousand Native Americans. This group called themselves Lenni-Lenape, which means "ordinary people." The Europeans called this group the Delaware because of the Delaware River that ran through the area. This is the name by which many people still know them. Mostly farmers, the Lenni-Lenape raised crops such as corn, beans, and squash. They also fished and hunted for meat.

These people lived undisturbed by Europeans until the 1500s. An Italian sailor, Giovanni da Verrazzano, touched the coast of New Jersey during an expedition for the French in 1524. But the French did not settle here, and the Lenni-Lenape were left alone for almost another century.

Then in 1609 an English explorer named Henry Hudson came to the area while on an expedition for the Dutch East India Company. Hudson sailed his ship

Sir George Carteret arrived in New Jersey in the mid-1660s. He had been given property rights to part of New Jersey by the Duke of York.

the *Half Moon* into what is now Newark Bay and up the river that was later named after him. A second explorer for the Dutch, Cornelius Mey, explored the southern half of the state. Both explorers liked what they saw, and the Netherlands claimed the land that the French had passed up. The area they called New Netherland included most of present-day New York, Delaware, Connecticut, and Pennsylvania, in addition to New Jersey.

In 1638 Swedish traders began to settle in southern New Jersey. By 1640 they had built two forts along the Delaware. But the Dutch didn't like any trading competition, so they forced the Swedes out in 1655. Then in 1660 the Dutch established Bergen, New Jersey's first permanent European settlement. By 1663 about two hundred Dutch settlers lived in the New Jersey area of New Netherland.

In August 1664 England sent a fleet of warships to the colony. The commander of the fleet demanded that the Dutch settlers surrender, which they did without firing a shot. The land was given to James, the Duke of York. James kept part of it for himself and named it New York. The rest of the land was awarded to his two friends, Sir George Carteret and Lord John Berkeley. The land was called New Jersey in honor of Carteret's birthplace, the Isle of Jersey.

Settlers came to New Jersey because property prices were low and for the chance to practice their own religion. A group of Baptists settled in the eastern half of the colony. Some Puritans came from Connecticut in 1666 and founded the city of Newark.

All these new settlers brought new diseases. Thousands of Lenni-Lenape died from measles, smallpox, and other European illnesses.

In 1674 Berkeley sold his share of New Jersey to members of a religious society called the Quakers. The Quakers, an organization of peaceful, humanitarian Christians, were persecuted in England. New Jersey was an ideal place for them to settle because the colony allowed freedom of religion.

The sale of the land caused the colony to be officially divided. Carteret's half was called East Jersey, and the Quakers' half was now West Jersey. Carteret tried unsuccessfully to make a profit from his half of the land. After Carteret died, his heirs sold East Jersey to another group of Quakers in 1682. It wasn't until 1702, when New Jersey's owners gave up trying to govern, that East Jersey and West Jersey were reunited into one royal colony. By this time, there were around three thousand Lenni-Lenape left in their former homeland.

New Jersey colonists had their own legislature, but it was headed by New York's governor. The colonists protested, and England eventually listened. Lewis Morris of Monmouth County was appointed as the first governor of New Jersey in 1738.

By the 1760s, New Jersey had about one hundred towns. The one hundred thousand or so colonists living there spent most of their time growing their

The Salem Oak is more than five hundred years old. John Fenwick, a Quaker settler, stood under the tree when he signed a peace treaty with the Lenni-Lenape in 1675.

own food and building homes. New Jersey was the only colony with two colleges. The College of New Jersey was founded in 1746. Ten years later the college was moved to Princeton. In 1896 it was renamed Princeton University. Queen's College was founded in 1766. Later it was renamed Rutgers University.

Like colonists all over the eastern coast, the people of New Jersey started to get upset about laws that they thought were unfair. By 1774 Great Britain had limited colonial trade and passed high taxes on items such as tea, glass, and paper.

Ford Mansion, in Morristown, was George Washington's headquarters for two winters of the Revolutionary War.

George Washington led his discouraged troops across the Delaware River into Trenton, New Jersey, on a stormy winter night in 1776. The next day they took the enemy by surprise and won their first major battle in the Revolutionary War.

Less than a year later, the Revolutionary War began. About twenty thousand New Jersey residents fought for independence over the course of the war's eight years. Because of its location between New York and Philadelphia, New Jersey was the battleground for over one hundred clashes between the American patriots and the British soldiers. The first major victory for the Continental Army was at the Battle of Trenton. One week later, in January 1777, the Americans surprised a British fort at Princeton. Another American victory occurred at Monmouth Courthouse in June 1778. In one of the largest battles of the war, Mary Hays, better known as Molly Pitcher, helped fire her wounded husband's cannon.

The British at last gave up the colonies in 1783. Four years later, New Jersey signed the Constitution and became the third state. In 1790 the New Jersey legislature allowed women who owned property to vote. This law was changed in 1807, however, when lawmakers claimed that women voters had determined the result of a close election.

Soon there were roads in New Jersey. By 1820 the state had built 550 miles of toll roads, more than any other state. Railroads and canals soon stretched across the land. With better transportation, iron ore from the northern hills could be carried to the factories in Paterson and Trenton. New Jersey was on its way to becoming the major industrial state that it is today.

When the Civil War began, New Jersey remained in the Union. The state had allowed slaves at first but passed a law in 1804 to gradually free them all. New Jersey was the last state to pass laws allowing slaves their freedom. About 88,000 New Jerseyans served in the Union Army. But some people in New Jersey still had a lot of sympathy for the South. In fact, New Jersey was one of only three states that voted against reelecting President Abraham Lincoln in 1864.

After the Civil War, industry boomed in New Jersey. By 1876 most of its residents lived within six miles of a railroad line. Much of the woods of the Lenni-Lenape were gone. In their place were factories.

Beginning in the 1880s, thousands of Europeans came to New Jersey to work in these factories. They made sewing machines, elevators, and steam locomotives. Many others worked in textile plants. In 1890 New Jerseyans numbered just under 1.5 million. By 1915— just 25 years later—this figure had doubled to almost three million. Most of these people lived in cities to be near the factories. In fact, by 1900, more than half of New Jersey's population lived in cities. Farms were disappearing rapidly from the Garden State.

In the 1800s Paterson became a center for silk production. The silk factory area was known as the Paterson Silk Mill District.

In 1910 New Jerseyans elected Woodrow Wilson by a large margin to be their governor. Wilson was born in Virginia but had lived in New Jersey as president of Princeton University. He helped the state legislature create laws to solve the new problems that came with the growth of industry. He cleaned up corruption in the state government and fought for the rights of workers who were injured on the job. Woodrow Wilson's success in New Jersey played a big part in his first election as President of the United States in 1912.

This was also the era in which Thomas Alva Edison worked in New Jersey. In 1876 he set up his first laboratory in Menlo Park. It was here that he invented the record player, or phonograph, and the electric light. Edison next moved to a larger laboratory at West Orange in 1887, where he made the first motion picture. Edison died in West Orange in 1931. He had patented 1,093 inventions during his lifetime, all of them made in New Jersey.

During World Wars I and II, the factories that had been crucial to the growth of New Jersey became crucial to the nation at war. They produced ammunition, airplanes, uniforms, and ships. It was because of World War II that more electronics and chemical companies came into the state around 1940.

After World War II, the economy boomed again. Many people moved from the cities to the suburbs, the communities around the cities. In 1952 the New Jersey Turnpike opened, connecting Philadelphia to New York City and providing suburban commuters with an easier route to work. But as people moved away from the cities, so did their tax money. This meant that

Thomas Edison worked with a home movie projector in his West Orange laboratory around 1900. Edison developed the first motion picture here in 1889.

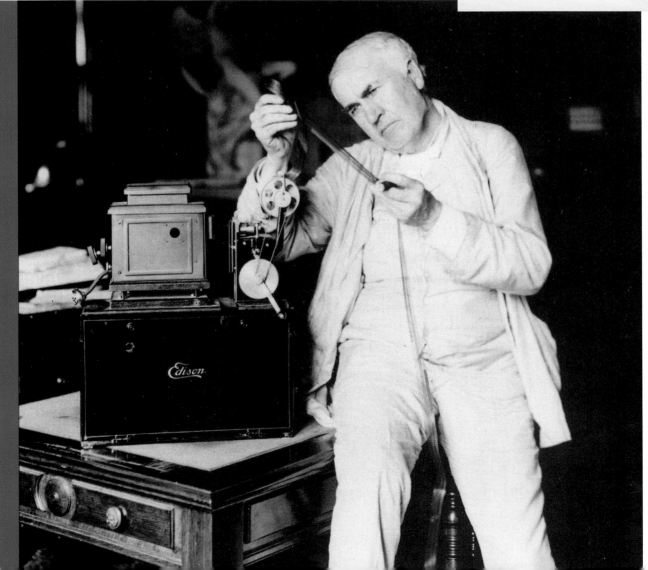

Men work on an assembly line in a Paterson factory during the 1940s.

cities could no longer afford to keep their schools, roads, and buildings in good shape.

The New Jersey government looked for new ways to raise money. They set up a lottery in the late 1960s. In 1976 New Jersey instituted a law that allowed gambling in Atlantic City. The money generated by gambling paid for new social programs in the state. These programs included state colleges, water conservation and purification, and urban renewal. Many problems in the cities are still growing faster than they can be fixed. One third of the people of Newark were living in poverty in 1992. Even worse, poverty affected two thirds of the children of Camden that year. But a new urban development plan, started in 1993, has improved some of these problems already.

Toxic waste disposal is another problem that New Jersey has been dealing with. In 1978 New Jersey created the first state-level department of energy in the United States. With new sources of energy, such as nuclear power, came new sources of pollution. So, in the 1980s the Department of Energy had to help find ways to dispose of the toxic waste. Unfortunately this problem and problems with disposal of other types of waste still trouble New Jersey today. But the many motivated and creative people in New Jersey, citizens and lawmakers alike, are ready to help tackle this and other problems.

The 137-mile New Jersey Turnpike is pictured as it looked when it first opened in 1952.

Lights! Camera! Action in New Jersey!

Think of a place famous for making movies. Most people would think of Hollywood, California. In fact, moviemaking began in West Orange, New Jersey. It all started in the laboratory of one of the world's greatest inventors.

You may think of Thomas Edison as the man who invented the light-bulb. He was also the inventor of the "talking machine," or phonograph. In 1877 Edison recorded himself reciting "Mary Had a Little Lamb." That was the very first recording. The phonograph was the first invention that allowed people to hear recorded sounds. People were very excited by the phonograph. Soon it became as popular as CD players are today.

Edison wanted to connect the phonograph to a moving-picture camera. He thought people would enjoy watching "talking pictures." He asked one of his laboratory assistants,

Thomas Edison adjusts an early theater projector.

Edison at first thought of his kinetoscope as little more than a toy. When it was demonstrated in New York City, however, it created a huge sensation, and kinetoscope parlors became very popular.

W.K.L. Dickson, to help. Dickson's specialty was photography. Many other inventors around the world were working on the idea of a motion-picture camera. Dickson studied what others were doing. Then he set out to invent his own camera to record movement.

Dickson worked long hours in the laboratory in West Orange. By 1893 he had it! His camera moved film forward so he could take one photo after another. When the film was played, the figures in the pictures appeared to be moving. Dickson called his motion-picture camera the Kinetograph. He named the machine that played the movies the Kinetoscope. He got the idea for these names from the Greek word *kinesis*. "Kinesis" means motion.

The Kinetoscope allowed one person at a time to see a movie. For 25 cents you entered a "Kinetoscope parlor." You looked through two lenses just as you would look through binoculars. These magnified the film. As you watched, the film moved across a light. Before your very eyes, black-and-white photographs were moving. The first movie made was of a man sneezing. Believe it or not, people couldn't wait to watch it.

Next, Edison acquired a projector invented by Thomas Armat. This projector, called the Vitascope, showed movies on a screen. Now many people could view a movie together. The movie theater was born! Unfortunately, Edison wasn't able to meet his original goal. He couldn't connect movies to the phonograph's sound as he had hoped. All the earliest movies were silent.

People were thrilled about the movies. Someone had to make more of them. Edison built "the Black Maria," the first movie studio. This was a one-room building that turned around on tracks. It takes bright light to film a

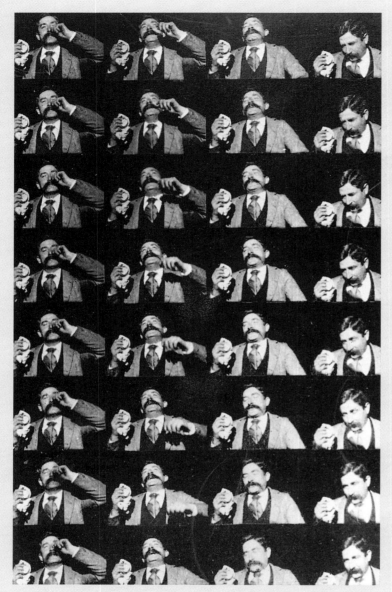
Edison's filmed sneeze, from about 1894, is thought to be the oldest copyrighted movie.

movie, so Edison's studio could be rotated to follow the movement of the sun. That way the filmmakers always had the brightest sunlight available.

Pretty soon the public wasn't satisfied watching a man sneeze. They grew tired of seeing a horse galloping by. Watching movement alone was no longer enough. Now they demanded stories. They wanted the movies to be more like stage plays.

Edison's company began to film stories in Fort Lee, New Jersey. They hired actors to play the characters. They tried to find interesting places to film the action. Costumes and sets became important. Moviemaking as we know it today had begun.

The earliest movie directors came to Fort Lee to make their films. Certain actors became popular with the public. The idea of "movie stars" was born. The movie star Douglas Fairbanks

Edison built the first movie studio, the Black Maria, near his West Orange laboratory in the mid-1890s.

acted in a film about the Old West. He rode his horse through a movie set of log cabins. Today, tollbooths for the George Washington Bridge stand on the spot where that set was.

Between 1890 and 1920, New Jersey's movie business grew. Universal, Goldwyn, Metro, Fox, and Paramount all made movies in Fort Lee. The Solax studio was headed by the world's first woman director, Alice Guy-Blanche.

When many companies all try to sell the same product, business gets competitive. Movie companies started fighting. Some companies began hiring gangsters to steal cameras and threaten movie crews. As things got worse, many movie companies decided to leave town. California offered bright sunlight and lots of good weather. Before long, Hollywood became the movie capital. Fort Lee, New Jersey, was forgotten.

In 1978 the New Jersey Motion Picture and Television Commission was created. This agency works to attract moviemakers back to New Jersey. The commission helps moviemakers find places to film movies. They help find supplies and workers needed for the movie. They've brought thousands of film and television projects to New Jersey. These projects have included feature films, television programs, music videos, short films, and commercials. Moviemaking will always be a part of New Jersey's history. Today, movies are a part of New Jersey's future as well.

Crossroads of the East

New Jersey packs a lot of life into a small package. There are a lot of cities, towns, and factories. And there are a lot of people. New Jersey is only the forty-sixth largest state in the union, but it ranks ninth in population. In fact, it is the most densely populated state in the country.

It's no wonder that most people think of New Jersey as a state full of cities. Almost ninety percent of New Jersey's population lives in urban areas. Only one other state matches that statistic—California, on the other side of the continent. And most of New Jersey's cities are bustling manufacturing spots like Camden, Newark, Paterson, and Trenton.

Thousands of New Jersey residents work outside of the state. This is because of New Jersey's location. Every morning the cars flow through the Holland and Lincoln tunnels and over the George Washington Bridge into New York City. Others drive across bridges on the Delaware River into Philadelphia. Crowded

On average, 995 people occupy each square mile of New Jersey. In Newark, New Jersey's largest city, more than 11,000 people occupy each square mile.

25

Water power from the 77-foot-high Paterson Falls, on the Passaic River, provides energy for Paterson's industry.

Both national and international trade take place in Port Newark, the busiest port in New Jersey.

commuter trains and buses stop frequently on their way into Philadelphia and New York.

It's hard to find better transportation than is available in this coastal state. Wharves line the New Jersey side of the Hudson River for miles. Great freighters and ocean liners sail up the Hudson and the Delaware rivers to dock in New Jersey. The New Jersey Turnpike links Philadelphia and New York City with almost 150 miles of highway. And the nation's first ferry service, which began running from Hoboken to Manhattan in 1811, is still used by thousands of commuters and visitors each day.

New Jersey's location makes it a vital part of the nation's transportation system. New Jerseyans have always known this—it was the first state to help local communities build roads. The first regular airplane passenger service in the country started in 1919 between Atlantic City and New York City. Today, Newark International Airport is one of the nation's busiest airports.

All of this transportation—air, rail, sea, and road—made New Jersey an ideal place for manufacturing. New Jersey was called "the workshop of the nation" because it produced so many manufactured products. Today, however, the products of New Jersey's factories account for only 17 percent of the value of goods produced in the state. Nevertheless, this small state still boasts over 15,000 factories. The three major manufactured products are chemicals, food products, and printed materials. Electrical machinery and equipment are also important.

New Jersey leads the nation in chemical manufacturing. They make everything from soap for your bathroom to wrinkle-free cloth for your clothes—from

The George Washington Bridge connects New York City with Fort Lee, New Jersey. To accommodate the huge number of vehicles traveling between the two states, the bridge has two levels and a total of 14 lanes.

paints to plastics to wonder drugs. There are about a thousand chemical plants in this small state. Most of them are either near the Hudson River or in an area extending from Newark to Camden.

Food processing is another type of manufacturing found in New Jersey. A food processing plant is where companies cook, can, freeze, and otherwise prepare food. One factory dries and bags tea from India. Another makes and freezes cakes made from wheat flour from the mills of the Midwest.

The third biggest industry in New Jersey is printed materials. Newspapers, books, and magazines are printed, bound, and sent all over the world.

But if you go past the factories and off the big highways, you'll see miles and miles of houses with green lawns and backyard barbecues. New Jersey is a land of suburbs. Many of the people who live in these suburbs work in New York, Connecticut, Pennsylvania, and Delaware. But not all of New Jersey's human resources leave the state to go to work. In fact, more and more people work within the state because of the rise in service industries. These are industries in which workers serve other people instead of making an actual product. Today more than three quarters of New Jersey's money comes from service industries. Finance, insurance, and real estate are the most important of these types of work. Education, health care, and retail trade are also crucial to New Jersey's changing economy. And don't forget about communications. Look on any AT&T pay phone, and you'll see that their headquarters is in Basking Ridge, New Jersey.

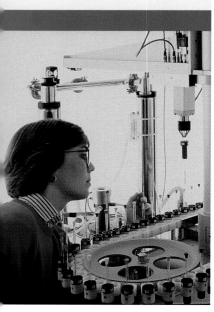

Many chemical companies have research facilities in New Jersey.

The tourist industry is also an important part of New Jersey's economy. Atlantic City attracts the most tourists in the state. Thousands of people each year visit the city's gambling casinos and walk along its famous boardwalk. Tourism brings in ten percent of New Jersey's profits.

Even in this crowded, busy state, there are still farms and forests. Three out of four of New Jersey's residents live north of Trenton. That means there is plenty of room in the southern part of the state for agriculture. There are about 8,500 small but very productive farms in New Jersey. Most are in the southern half of the state. There are plenty of trees, too. Almost forty percent of the state is forest.

A Bell Labs technician is using laser light to test optical glass-fibers.

You won't see acres and acres of corn and wheat grown here—agriculture accounts for less than one percent of New Jersey's income. But amazingly, as small as these farms are, the production of ten of New Jersey's fruit and vegetable crops ranks among the top eight in the nation. And millions of roses, orchids, geraniums, lilies, and other types of flowers come from New Jersey's greenhouses. New Jersey's nickname of "the Garden State" still applies.

New Jersey's location is important for its farmers, too. They grow the fresh fruits and vegetables that feed the people in the big cities along the East Coast. The small farmers and gardeners of New Jersey work hard to see that that population can bite into fresh New Jersey fruits and vegetables as often as they like.

A Forty-Eight Acre Horn of Plenty

There used to be a lot more farms in New Jersey. But for twenty years after World War II, the state lost about one farm a day. That's more than seven thousand farms. The land was just too valuable; there were factories and housing developments to be built.

But a handful of farmers still refuse to give up their land. George Kuehm and his family are one example. Four generations of Kuehms have farmed fruits and vegetables on their 48 acres of land. Now, theirs is one of the last farms in Passaic County, just twenty-five miles from New York City. "When my father was farming, it was mainly all farms in this area," Kuehm recalls. "There weren't any developments around. Now we're in the middle of a city, I would say."

The Kuehms own what is called a truck farm, a farm that grows vegetables, fruits, or both to sell. Many of these farms do use trucks to transport their goods, but this is not where they got their name. *Truck* used to mean "to barter or trade," so farmers who traded their produce at urban markets began to be called truck farmers. This is why many farmers who now use air or rail transport—and no trucks at all—are still called truck farmers.

New Jersey is one of the leading producers of cranberries.

A small roadside fruit-and-vegetable market offers New Jersey-grown produce such as sweet corn, tomatoes, cucumbers, and peaches.

Most truck farms are fairly small because fruit and vegetable crops don't take up as much land as grain crops. The amount of food produced on such small plots is amazing. On a single acre, for example, the Kuehms raise 15,000 quarts of strawberries a year.

Most of the produce from New Jersey truck farms is sold to buyers from New York and Philadelphia. Or it's sold to the factories that prepare food, turning tomatoes into spaghetti sauce and fruit into filling for frozen pies. Many farmers also sell to their neighbors at a roadside stand or at a nearby farmers' market.

Land in Passaic County can be sold for as much as fifty thousand dollars an acre. It would be easy for these farmers to sell their land, but their family tradition is important to

Farm workers harvest pumpkins from a New Jersey field.

them. As George Kuehm explains, "My grandfather bought this farm, and my uncle and my father took over. My father passed away, and I took over his part, and it's been handed down from generation to generation . . . and I'd like to see it stay this way."

31

A State Filled with Contrasts

The land, the history, and the people of New Jersey are filled with contrasts. Huge chemical plants live side by side with woodlands. Scenic mountains are a few miles drive from the sandy beaches of the Atlantic Ocean. The modern buildings and flashing lights of Atlantic City seem to clash with New Jersey's more traditional cultural offerings, such as the state Shakespeare Festival, the Chamber Symphony of Princeton, and the yearly production of *The Nutcracker* at the Paper Mill Playhouse in Millburn.

New Jersey's literary history is just as diverse. At one end of the literary rainbow is William Carlos Williams who was born in Rutherford. One of his most famous works was *Paterson*, a book-length poem about the growth of industry in that New Jersey city.

At the other end is Walt Whitman, another great American poet, who lived for several years in Camden. Unlike Williams, Whitman's works are very descriptive, almost flowery. Whitman's home in New Jersey is now a museum.

The Mid-Atlantic Center for the Arts in Cape May offers tours of the city's landmarks, including many Victorian-style homes.

The Paper Mill Playhouse's production of the *Wizard of Oz* featured spectacular sets and costumes. The theater is housed in a converted paper mill in Millburn.

In between these two writers, you'll find Stephen Crane. Born in Newark, Crane wrote the beautiful novel *The Red Badge of Courage* about a young man's struggle in the Civil War. He also wrote more than one hundred short stories, two volumes of poetry, and five other novels. Stephen Crane was only 28 years old when he died.

New Jersey's 130-mile coastline is perfect for the wide range of recreational water activities enjoyed by residents and visitors.

You'll find vast differences among New Jersey musicians also. Pianist, composer, and big band leader Count Basie was born here, as were singers Sarah Vaughan and Frank Sinatra. Pop and rock stars such as Bruce Springsteen, Whitney Houston, Paul Simon, and Jon Bon Jovi produce various musical sounds. But these modern artists and their classic counterparts grew from the same musical roots in New Jersey.

Paul Robeson, one of the first world-recognized African American actors, was born in Princeton. He was not only a radio and movie actor, but he also performed on the stage. The comedy team of Bud Abbott and Lou Costello got their start here. And two of today's finest actors, Meryl Streep and Jack Nicholson, also hail from New Jersey.

New Jersey has been called the workshop of the nation, but it is also the playground of the East Coast. Much of New Jersey's coastline consists of a long, narrow sandbar lined with resort cities. Cape May, at

Bruce Springsteen was born and raised in Freehold, New Jersey. By the mid-1980s Springsteen and his group, the E Street Band, had achieved international fame.

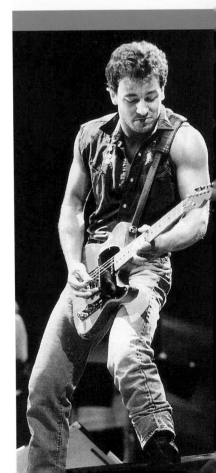

New Jersey's southernmost tip, lays claim to being the nation's first seaside resort. One 17-block section of the town is made up of beautiful old Victorian buildings. The big wooden hotels with their gingerbread trim and wide porches bring back the quiet charm of another time.

Cape May's partner in contrast is Atlantic City. Built on a narrow, sandy island that stretches four miles out into the Atlantic Ocean, Atlantic City was land that wasn't much good for anything. There was no fresh water and nothing grew. But it was close to the cities, where in the hot summers people were hungry for a little fresh air and cool ocean. So in 1878, the city built the world's first boardwalk. The 4½-mile Boardwalk along the Atlantic Ocean was lined with

Even though Atlantic City's Boardwalk is sixty feet wide, it can become very crowded in the evenings when people arrive to visit the city's nightclubs, restaurants, and casinos.

Lucy the Margate Elephant was built in 1881 to attract real estate buyers to the Atlantic City area. Today Lucy is a national historic landmark.

hotels, shops, and restaurants. Soon Atlantic City became a popular resort area.

Atlantic City's Boardwalk was always filled with crowds—and anything that would bring more crowds. There was a horse that dove off a tall tower into a swimming pool. There were sidewalk artists and entertainers. There were funhouses and roller coasters. Atlantic City was lights and noise and fun.

When it became easy for tourists of nearby cities to fly to more distant resorts, Atlantic City fell on hard times. Its beach could not compete with the vast stretches of Florida sand. Then in 1976, when the state of New Jersey made gambling legal in the old resort, Atlantic City began booming again. The Boardwalk is busy once more with crowds of tourists.

The board game Monopoly is based on Atlantic City.

The game of Monopoly was inspired by Atlantic City. The street names on the game board are real streets of the city. And these days, everybody wants a hotel on Boardwalk.

Over One Million Acres of Beauty

Who would have thought that the largest wilderness area east of the Mississippi would be found in New Jersey? Most of southern New Jersey, however—over one million acres of it—is part of the New Jersey Pinelands, or Pine Barrens. This huge national reserve is a beautiful, wild, natural place, filled with pine trees, farmlands, and rivers.

The Pinelands are home to more than 1,200 plant and animal species, almost one hundred of which are endangered. About twenty years ago, the federal government recognized the need to preserve this rich, diverse area. They established the Pinelands as the nation's first national reserve in 1978. The next year, New Jersey enacted the Pinelands Protection Act to place very strict rules on the way this land could be used. This act set up a 15-member

Egrets are one of the many kinds of birds that are found in the Pinelands. Although egrets came near extinction at one time, wildlife reserves such as the Pinelands have helped to save them.

"Wetlands," areas where underground water reaches the surface, cover about one quarter of the Pinelands.

These forests may be called the Pine Barrens, but they're full of life. Over 1,200 species of plants and animals live here.

The Rose Pogonia Orchid is an endangered plant that grows in the Pinelands.

Pinelands Commission to make sure that these rules would be followed.

There are many things in the Pinelands that need protection and preservation besides plants and animals. For example, beneath this area runs a 17-trillion gallon groundwater source. That's enough to cover New Jersey with ten feet of water. Many people get their drinking water from this source, so it must be kept free of pollution. The Pinelands are also a valuable source of natural history. Over one thousand prehistoric sites have been found here, some with fossils dating as far back as 10,000 B.C. In addition, most of New Jersey's blueberry and cranberry farms, important to the state's economy, are located within the Pinelands.

Government commissions aside, it's the people of the Pinelands who are most concerned about preserving the land. Like the Native Americans who lived in New Jersey hundreds of years ago, they love and respect this wilderness. Leo Landy is one of these residents. He has lived in the Pinelands for over fifty years.

"Everybody's got to have a place left to get out and stretch and get to know themselves a little better, and if you're crowded up like sardines, I don't see how you're going to do it." With the help of the Pinelands Commission, people will always be able to enjoy this special part of New Jersey.

Taking Action for a Clean Ocean

A garden club and surfing association have banded together. The Girl Scouts and a group of chefs have joined them. Teachers, business groups, women's clubs, and members of the fishing industry have come aboard. Why are all these people working together? They are part of Clean Ocean Action in Highlands, New Jersey. They are trying to stop pollution along Atlantic Ocean beaches.

Over 175 different groups have united to form Clean Ocean Action. These groups represent thousands of people working to make the Atlantic Ocean clean and safe. They know that careless people cause much of ocean pollution. Clean Ocean Action wants people to stop polluting.

When pollution comes from many unrelated sources, it is called "pointless pollution." Environmentalists think pointless pollution may cause at least half of America's water pollution. Pointless pollution is very hard to control because it comes from so many places. Clean Ocean Action is making people more aware of pointless pollution.

Anything that goes down a storm drain reaches a sewer. Much of what reaches the sewers eventually reaches the ocean. Every time it rains, oil and gasoline are washed down storm drains

Sixth graders stencil a visual reminder next to a storm drain to remind people that everything entering the drain will eventually reach a river, a lake, or an ocean.

to the sewers. Animal waste, litter, and lawn chemicals are rushed toward the ocean the same way. Add to that poisons found in batteries, paints, and household cleaners. Without knowing it, we are all contributing to pointless pollution. One gallon of oil dumped down a storm drain can create an eight-acre oil slick. It may pollute up to one million gallons of drinking water! Clean Ocean Action wants people to know all these facts.

Clean Ocean Action's logo is part of their campaign to alert people to the problem of pointless pollution.

It is easy to see why Clean Ocean Action is so concerned. They know that only 28 percent of New Jersey's ocean waters are fishable and swim-mable. They have seen one half of New Jersey's clam beds closed because of disease. They know thousands of animals die from being caught in, or from eating, plastic. They have read the results of tests on water, mud, and waste. They realize that unless pollution stops, the oceans will be poisonous.

One way in which Clean Ocean Action is helping to stop pointless pollution is by "painting the town blue." This project leads students on a storm-drain stenciling activity. Students use a stencil to paint a picture of a blue fish near storm drains. The fish reminds the public that everything that goes down the storm drain affects ocean life.

The people of Clean Ocean Action take action in many other ways, too. They publish a monthly newsletter and many educational booklets. Members work to get the word out to the public. Each spring and fall they hold a beach clean-up. Volunteers get hands-on experience removing litter and waste from the coastline. They campaign to make public officials aware of the problems. They push to see that environmental laws are followed. Because of Clean Ocean Action's members, New Jersey's waters are getting better.

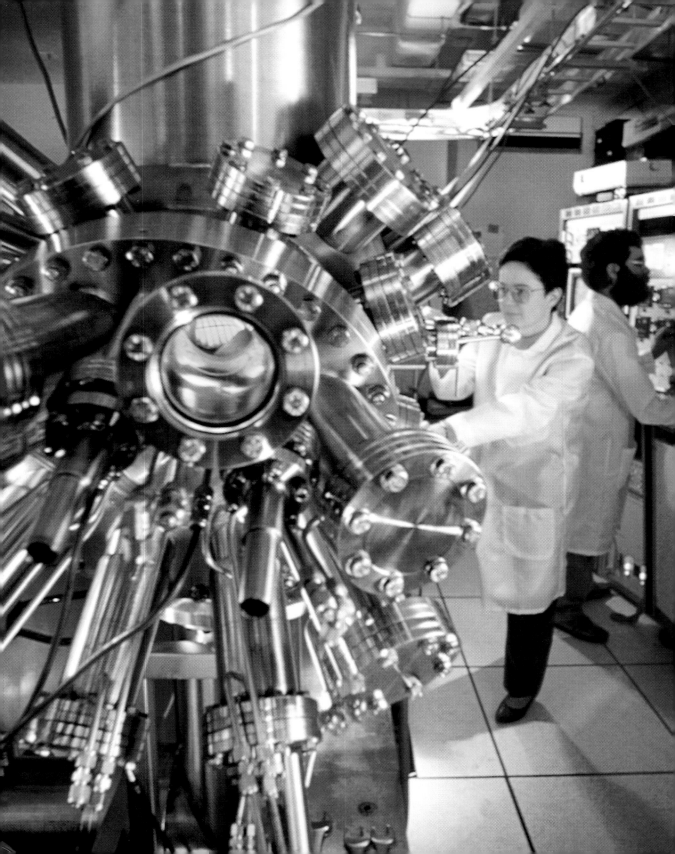

"What a Difference a State Makes"

New Jersey has always been a leader in progress. Thomas Edison invented the electric light and the record player in a laboratory in Menlo Park. For many years Albert Einstein worked and taught at the Institute of Advanced Study in Princeton. These men, two of the world's greatest scientists and inventors, found New Jersey a good place to experiment and prepare for the future.

Today, researchers across the state carry on that tradition. AT&T Bell Laboratories has developed the laser, the solar cell, and the transistor in New Jersey. And they're not the only ones exploring new ideas in New Jersey. In fact, ten percent of the nation's research dollars are spent here. The state's 140,000 scientists, engineers, and skilled technicians give it the highest concentration of brainpower in the nation.

But where exactly is all this research leading? As Arno Penzias, who won a Nobel Prize for his work at Bell Labs, explains, "Our abilities will be able to meet the needs of the future without having to find more

New Jersey's AT&T Bell Laboratories is one of the most well-respected industrial research labs in the world.

Albert Einstein was one of the first professors at Princeton University's Institute of Advanced Studies.

farmland or more iron ore or more petroleum—all the things that the planet is running out of. We're going to try to replace those physical resources with mental resources, do things with ingenuity."

Ingenuity, a skill or cleverness, is a word that fits the people of New Jersey well. Just ask the farmers who have used their handful of acres to place the state second in the nation's production of blueberries and third in production of cranberries. Just ask the people of the Pinelands who have lived for generations on the fish from their streams, the wild animals from their woods, and even the area's vegetation, such as huckle-berries.

But New Jersey is looking for some cleverness and skill in controlling one future problem. Many states all over the country are dealing with pollution, over-crowding, and the high costs of government. As a state with so many factories and cities, New Jersey is no exception to these problems.

In cities like Paterson, factories and mills have closed. Where there were once thriving cities, there are now communities working with dedication and ingenuity to save their past and create a new life. Some of the fine old buildings that housed industry in the past are being remade into offices, shops, and apartment buildings.

New Jersey's new motto, "What a Difference a State Makes" reflects this state's confidence and positive attitude. With its energy, diversity, and devel-opmental resources, it is well prepared to face new challenges.

Important Historical Events

1524 Giovanni da Verrazzano, an Italian navigator sailing for the French, explores the New Jersey coast. New Jersey is inhabited at this time by Native Americans called the Lenni-Lenape.

1609 Henry Hudson explores the Sandy Hook Bay area and sails up the Hudson River for the Dutch East India Company.

1614 Cornelius Mey sails the Delaware River.

1638 Swedish settlers and traders settle along the Delaware River.

1660 The Dutch build a permanent settlement in Bergen, now part of Jersey City.

1664 The English win control of New Jersey from the Dutch.

1674 A group of Quakers buys part of New Jersey. Two years later the colony is divided into West Jersey and East Jersey.

1702 England combines East and West Jersey into a single royal colony.

1738 Lewis Morris becomes New Jersey's first royal governor.

1776 New Jersey adopts its first constitution. Washington crosses the Delaware on Christmas night and the next day defeats a Hessian army in Trenton.

1787 On December 18 New Jersey becomes the third state to ratify the Constitution.

1793 Jean-Pierre Blanchard takes the first balloon flight in America, to deliver a letter for George Washington.

1804 Alexander Hamilton is killed in a duel with Vice President Aaron Burr at Weehawken.

1825 The first steam locomotive in the United States is built at Hoboken by John Stevens.

1844 New Jersey adopts its second constitution.

1845 Charles C. Stratton becomes the first governor of New Jersey elected directly by the voters rather than chosen by the legislature.

1869 Rutgers defeats the College of New Jersey (now Princeton) in New Brunswick in the nation's first college football game.

1879 Thomas A. Edison invents the electric light bulb in Menlo Park.

1889 Edison develops the motion picture in West Orange.

1910 Woodrow Wilson is elected governor of New Jersey.

1919 On May 3 the first airline passenger service begins, running from Atlantic City to New York City.

1940 Les Paul invents the first solid body electric guitar in Mahwah.

1947 New Jersey adopts its third constitution.

1952 The New Jersey Turnpike opens, linking Philadelphia and New York.

1969 New Jersey voters approve a state lottery to raise money for schools and state government.

1976 New Jersey adopts an income tax. A referendum that permits gambling casinos in Atlantic City is passed. The Meadowlands Sports Complex opens in East Rutherford.

1993 A statewide urban development project is begun.

The state flag shows a version of the state seal on a field of yellow. The seal shows a shield with three plows, symbolizing agriculture. On the right of the shield stands Ceres, the goddess of agriculture. Liberty stands on the left side. The helmet represents New Jersey's sovereignty. A horse's head above the helmet stands for strength, speed, and usefulness.

New Jersey Almanac

Nickname. The Garden State

Capital. Trenton

State Bird. Eastern goldfinch

State Flower. Purple violet

State Tree. Red oak

State Mottoes. Liberty and prosperity (original); What a Difference a State Makes!

State Song. No official song

State Abbreviations. N.J. (traditional); NJ (postal)

Statehood. December 18, 1787, the 3rd state

Government. Congress: U.S. senators, 2; U.S. representatives, 13. State Legislature: senators, 40; assembly members, 80. Counties: 21

Area. 7,790 sq mi (20,175 sq km), 46th in size among the states

Greatest Distances. north/south, 167 mi (268 km); east/west, 88 mi (142 km). Coastline: 130 mi (209 km)

Elevation. Highest: 1,803 ft (550 m). Lowest: sea level, along the Atlantic Ocean

Population. 1990 Census: 7,748,634 (5.2% increase over 1980), 9th among the states. Density: 995 persons per sq mi (384 persons per sq km). Distribution: 89% urban, 11% rural. 1980 Census: 7,364,158

Economy. *Agriculture:* greenhouse and nursery products, milk, tomatoes, peaches, cranberries, blueberries. *Fishing:* clams, flounder, lobster, menhaden. *Manufacturing:* chemicals, food products, printed materials, scientific instruments, electric equipment. *Mining:* crushed stone, sand and gravel

State Seal

State Flower: Purple violet
State Bird: Eastern goldfinch

Annual Events

★ New Jersey Flower and Garden Show in Somerset (February)

★ Native American Indian Pow-Wow in Belvedere (May)

★ New Jersey Renaissance Festival in Somerset (June)

★ New Jersey Festival of Ballooning in Readington (July)

★ State Fair in Cherry Hill (August)

★ Miss America Pageant in Atlantic City (September)

★ New Jersey State Ethnic Festival in Jersey City (September)

★ Reenactment of Washington Crossing the Delaware in Titusville (Christmas Day)

Places to Visit

★ Burlington Historic District

★ Delaware Water Gap

★ Liberty State Park in Jersey City

★ Edison's laboratory in Menlo Park

★ Morristown National Historical Park

★ New Jersey State Aquarium in Camden

★ Pine Barrens Village in Batsto

★ Seaside resorts (such as Seaside Heights, Wildwood, Atlantic City, Cape May, Ocean City)

★ Waterloo Village in Stanhope

Index